crochet purses

&accessories

Anne Rouzier & Vidlan Uckardes

D1709859

STACKPOLE BOOKS

0 11557 01434 1

CONTENTS

They say that fashion is a perpetual cycle that keeps repeating itself. This rule is true of crochet as well. And when crochet combines trendy with a pinch of nostalgia . . . you get the great accessories in this book, classic styles that have been updated to suit modern tastes. Colorful and easy to make, the purses, hats, and other accessories in this book compose an array of options for any occasion.

For those who haven't yet tried crochet or who need a refresher, the first section of this book goes over the basic stitches step by step. These pages also have the symbols used for these stitches in the stitch charts that are given for every project—plus small stitch charts and the stitches they describe to help you get used to reading charts.

Try out these 25 fun and functional projects and experience the satisfaction of wearing your own handiwork.

CROCHET STITCHES AND CHART SYMBOLS

HAND POSITION

How to hold the yarn

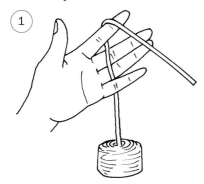

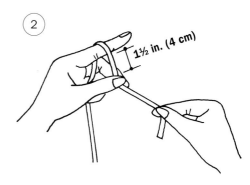

Bring the end of the yarn in front of the palm of the left hand, then bring the end attached to the skein or ball (called the "working yarn") up and around the index finger, between the index finger and the middle finger, and finally between the ring finger and the pinky finger.

Hold the tail end of the yarn between your thumb and middle finger, and raise your index finger about 1½ in. (4 cm) to hold up the yarn. This finger will move freely in order to control the tension on the yarn.

How to hold the hook

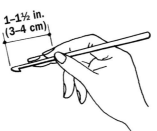

MAKING A SLIP KNOT

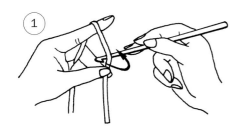

Start with the crochet hook behind the yarn. Bring it around in the direction of the arrrow.

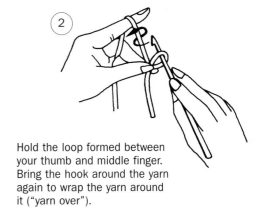

Hold the loop formed between your thumb and middle finger. Bring the hook around the yarn again to wrap the yarn around it ("yarn over").

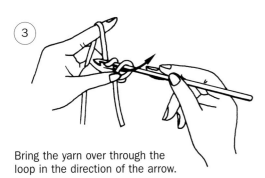

Bring the yarn over through the loop in the direction of the arrow.

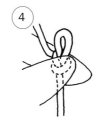

Hold the loop while pulling on the end of the yarn to tighten the base of the loop.

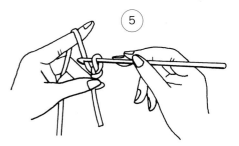

The slip knot formed is the base that all other crochet stitches start from.

STARTING ROWS

Each stitch has a height. Each row begins with a number of chains corresponding to the height of the stitches in that row. These chains are usually counted as the corresponding stitch (2 chains count as a half double crochet, 3 chains count as a double crochet, etc.). In the case of single crochet, when the row begins with a single chain, the chain does not count as a stitch.

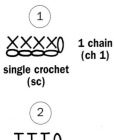

① 1 chain (ch 1)

single crochet (sc)

② 3 chains (ch 3)

double crochet (dc)

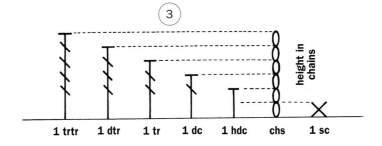

③

height in chains

1 trtr   1 dtr   1 tr   1 dc   1 hdc   chs   1 sc

STARTING A ROUND WITH A MAGIC RING

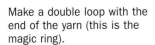

① Make a double loop with the end of the yarn (this is the magic ring).

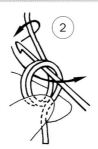

② Insert the hook through the ring and yarn over. Bring the yarn back through the ring in the direction of the arrow.

③ Yarn over again and draw the yarn through the loop you brought back through the ring.

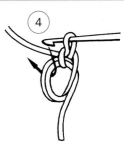

④ The stitch just formed serves as the chain stitch to begin a round of single crochet.

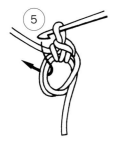

⑤ Work the number of single crochets indicated in the pattern, working through the ring.

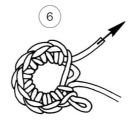

⑥ When you have finished all the stitches of the first round, tighten the ring by pulling the yarn end in the direction of the arrow.

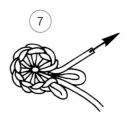

⑦ Continue pulling until the ring is tight.

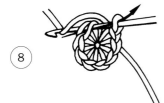

⑧ At the end of the round, insert the hook into the first single crochet and work a slip stitch to join the round.

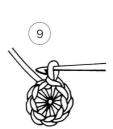

⑨ The first round (here, 8 single crochets) is completed.

STARTING A ROUND WITH A RING OF CHAINS

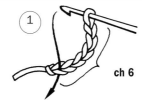

ch 6

Work the number of chains indicated in the pattern (here, 6 chains), then insert the hook into the first chain.

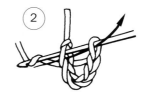

Yarn over, then draw the yarn through the chain and the loop on the hook to work a slip stitch.

The central ring is ready.

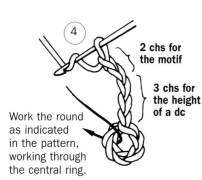

2 chs for the motif

3 chs for the height of a dc

Work the round as indicated in the pattern, working through the central ring.

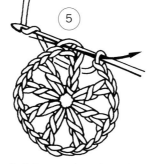

At the end of the round, work a slip stitch in the 3rd ch of the beginning ch-5 (the top of the chs representing the first dc).

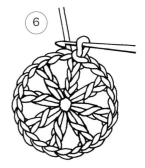

The first round is completed.

⬭ CHAIN STITCH (ch)

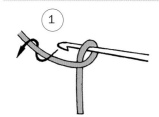

Start by making a slip knot: Wrap the yarn around the hook, then yarn over.

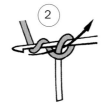

Draw the yarn back through the loop on the hook and pull to tighten the knot.

Yarn over, then draw the yarn back through the slip knot.

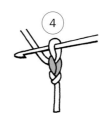

1 chain stitch completed.

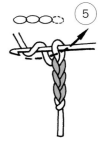

Continue in this manner until the required number of chains have been formed.

✕ SINGLE CROCHET (sc)

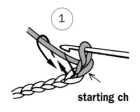

starting ch

Start the row of single crochet by working 1 ch. Insert the hook in the second chain from the hook (skipping the starting chain), yarn over, and draw the yarn back through the stitch—2 loops on hook.

Yarn over again, following the arrow.

Draw the yarn back through both loops on the hook.

1 single crochet completed.

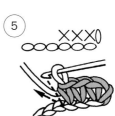

3 single crochets completed.

SLIP STITCH (sl st)

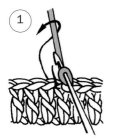

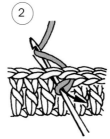

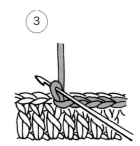

Insert the crochet hook under both strands of the stitch and yarn over by bringing the hook under and around the yarn in the direction of the arrow.

Pull the yarn back through the stitch and through the loop on the hook.

Slip stitch completed. Repeat steps 1 and 2 to work more slip stitches.

HALF DOUBLE CROCHET (hdc)

2 chs = the height of a hdc

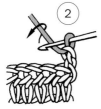

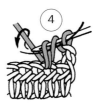

Prepare for a row of half double crochet by working two chains to stand in for the first half double crochet.

Turn the work. Yarn over, moving the hook in the direction of the arrow.

Insert the hook under both strands of the second stitch from the hook, yarn over, then drawn the yarn back through the stitch—3 loops on hook.

Yarn over and draw the yarn through all 3 loops on the hook—1 loop on hook.

Half double crochet completed.

3 half double crochets completed.

DOUBLE CROCHET (dc)

3 chs = the height of a dc

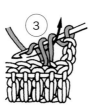

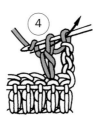

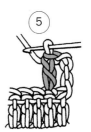

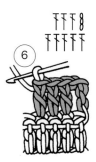

To prepare for a row of double crochet, chain 3 to stand in for the first double crochet.

Turn the work. Yarn over, insert the hook under both strands of the second stitch from the hook, yarn over again, and pull up a loop—3 loops on hook.

Yarn over and draw the yarn through the first two loops on the hook—2 loops on hook.

Yarn over again and draw the yarn through the two remaining loops—1 loop on hook.

Double crochet completed.

4 double crochets completed.

TREBLE CROCHET (tr)

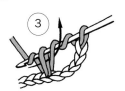

To prepare for a row of treble crochet, chain 4 to stand in for the first treble crochet.

Yarn over twice, insert the hook into the 6th chain from the hook, yarn over again, and pull up a loop—4 loops on hook.

Yarn over and draw the yarn through the first two loops on the hook, following the arrow—3 loops on hook.

Yarn over and draw the yarn through two more loops—2 loops on hook.

Yarn over again and draw the yarn through the two remaining loops—1 loop on hook.

4 treble crochets completed.

DOUBLE TREBLE (dtr)

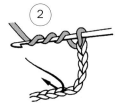

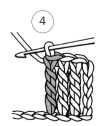

To prepare for a row of double treble crochet, chain 5 to stand in for the first double treble.

Yarn over three times, insert the hook into the 7th chain from the hook, yarn over again, and pull up a loop—5 loops on hook.

Yarn over and draw the yarn through two loops. Repeat this action 3 more times, until only 1 loop remains and the double treble is completed.

4 double trebles completed (the beginning ch-5 stands in for the first double treble).

FRONT POST DOUBLE CROCHET (fpdc)

Yarn over, then insert the hook around the post of the stitch of the previous row from front to back to front, as indicated by the arrow.

Yarn over and draw up a loop around the stitch. Complete the double crochet as normal: Yarn over and draw through two loops, then yarn over again and draw through the remaining two loops.

Front post double crochet completed.

BACK POST DOUBLE CROCHET (bpdc)

Yarn over, then insert the hook around the post of the stitch of the previous row from back to front to back, as indicated by the arrow.

Yarn over and draw up a loop around the stitch. Complete the double crochet as normal: Yarn over and draw through two loops, then yarn over again and draw through the remaining two loops.

Back post double crochet completed.

 Attach yarn

 Fasten off and cut yarn

 Insert the hook into the stitch indicated by this symbol

2 SINGLE CROCHETS IN THE SAME STITCH

Work 1 single crochet in the next stitch of the previous row, then insert the hook into the same stitch again.

Yarn over, pull up a loop, then yarn over again and pull through both loops on the hook.

2 single crochets in the same stitch completed.

SINGLE CROCHET 2 TOGETHER (sc2tog)

Insert the hook into the next stitch of the previous row, yarn over, and pull up a loop. Do not finish the single crochet, but insert the hook in the *next* stitch of the previous row and draw up a loop again—3 loops on the hook.

Yarn over and draw the yarn through all 3 loops on the hook.

Single crochet 2 together completed.

DOUBLE CROCHET 2 TOGETHER (dc2tog)

Start with an incomplete double crochet: Yarn over, insert the hook into the stitch, and draw up a loop; yarn over and draw through 2 loops. Do not finish the stitch.

Yarn over and insert the hook into the next stitch and work another incomplete double crochet as before—3 loops on the hook.

Yarn over and draw the yarn through all 3 loops on the hook.

Double crochet 2 together completed.

DOUBLE CROCHET 3 TOGETHER (dc3tog)

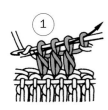 

Work an incomplete double crochet in each of the next 3 stitches of the previous round—4 loops on the hook. Yarn over and draw the yarn through all 4 loops.

Double crochet 3 together completed.

2 DOUBLE CROCHETS IN THE SAME STITCH

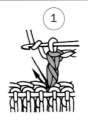 

Work 1 double crochet in the next stitch as normal, then yarn over and insert the hook in the same stitch. Complete the second double crochet as normal.

2 double crochet in the same stitch completed.

CH-3 PICOT (on a stitch)

  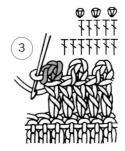

Chain 3, then insert the hook into the top of the stitch at the base of the chains, making sure to go under both strands of the stitch.

Yarn over and draw the yarn through the stitch and through the loop on the hook.

3 ch-3 picots (separated by double crochets) completed.

CH-3 PICOT (on a chain loop)

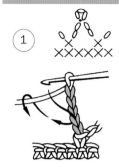

(1) Chain 5, then insert the hook into the 4th chain from the hook, as indicated by the arrow.

(2) Yarn over and draw the yarn through the stitch and the loop on the crochet hook.

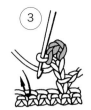

(3) The picot is completed. To complete the chain loop, ch 2, then insert the hook into the stitch indicated in the pattern for the end of the loop.

(4) Sc in that stitch. Ch-3 picot on chain loop completed.

Y STITCH

(1) Work a treble crochet in the stitch, then chain 2. Yarn over, then insert the hook into the post of the treble crochet, under two strands of the first pass through (the bottom "lump" on the post), and draw up a loop—3 loops on the hook.

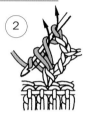

(2) Yarn over and draw through the first two loops on the hook; yarn over again and draw through the remaining two loops.

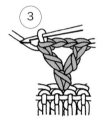

(3) Y stitch completed.

INVERTED Y STITCH

(1) Yarn over twice. Insert the hook into the stitch, yarn over, and draw up a loop. Yarn over again and draw the yarn through the first two loops on the stitch (incomplete dc formed)—3 loops on hook.

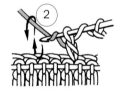

(2) Yarn over again, skip 2 stitches and insert the hook into the third stitch from the worked stitch. Draw up a loop, yarn over, and draw through two loops to form another incomplete dc—4 loops on hook.

(3) Yarn over and draw through the first two loops on the hook; yarn over again and draw through two loops; yarn over a third time and draw through the two remaining loops.

(4) Inverted Y stitch completed.

REVERSE SINGLE CROCHET (rev sc)

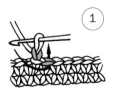

(1) Reverse single crochet is worked from left to right. Insert the hook into the first stitch to the right, as indicated by the arrow.

(2) Bring the hook up and over the working yarn to yarn over; draw up a loop through the stitch.

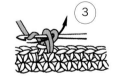

(3) Yarn over and draw the yarn through two loops.

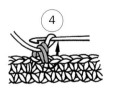

(4) Insert the hook into the next stitch to the right and repeat steps 1–3.

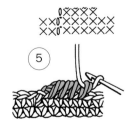

(5) Reverse single crochet is often used on the last row of a piece for edging.

HDC BOBBLE

1

Work an incomplete half double crochet in the stitch as follows: Yarn over, insert the hook into the stitch, and draw up a loop.

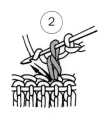

2

Repeat twice in the same stitch to make 3 incomplete half double crochets—7 loops on the hook. Yarn over and draw the yarn through all 7 loops.

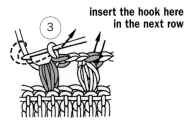

3

insert the hook here in the next row

Chain 1 to close up the bobble.

 ## DC BOBBLE

1

Work an incomplete double crochet as follows: Yarn over, insert the hook into the stitch, draw up a loop, yarn over, and draw through 2 loops.

2

Work 2 more incomplete double crochets in the same stitch—4 loops on the hook.

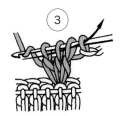

3

Yarn over and draw the yarn through all 4 loops.

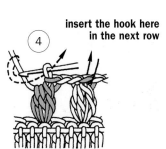

4

insert the hook here in the next row

Chain 1 to close up the bobble.

 ## POPCORN STITCH

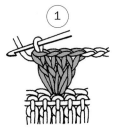

1

Work 4 double crochets in the same stitch.

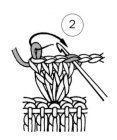

2

Carefully remove the hook from the working loop and insert it into the top of the first of the four double crochets.

3

Pick up the working loop again and draw it through the stitch.

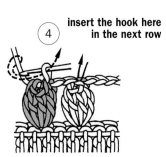

4

insert the hook here in the next row

Chain 1 to close up the popcorn stitch.

GUMDROPS

GUMDROPS

Front

YARN: Superfine (weight category 1) cotton yarn, 1 skein (150 yd/137 m; 1.5 oz./43 g) each in: green, pink, orange, blue, red, aqua, and natural.

HOOK: U.S. size D-3 (3.25 mm) crochet hook

NOTIONS: 30 in. (71 cm) sparkly ribbon; 1 beige curtain tie; 16 in. (41 cm) canvas fabric for the lining

FINISHED MEASUREMENTS: 14 by 11 by 2¼ in. (36 by 28 by 6 cm)

GAUGE: Side = 11 by 2¼ in. (28 by 6 cm)

PATTERN

With orange, ch 80. **Row 1:** Sc tbl in second ch from hook and in each ch across—79 sts. Turn. **Row 2:** With green, ch 1, sc tbl in each st across—79 sts. Turn. **Row 3:** With natural, ch 1, sc tbl in each st across—79 sts. Turn. **Rows 4–69:** Continue the work as indicated in the chart. Fasten off.

SIDE (MAKE 2)

With red, ch 10. **Row 1:** Ch 3 (counts as first dc), dc tbl in 5th ch from hook and in each ch across—10 sts. Turn. **Rows 2–24:** Ch 3, dc tbl in second st from hook and in each st across—10 sts. Fasten off.

FINISHING: Fold the large piece in half and attach the sides to it with a row of single crochet in red along each seam.

Make a lining from the canvas fabric the same size as the bag and sew it to the inside of the bag with very small stitches. Sew the handle to the ends of the opening.

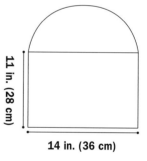

11 in. (28 cm)

14 in. (36 cm)

Back

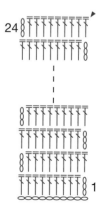

Side
foundation chain = 10 chs
(make 2 in red)

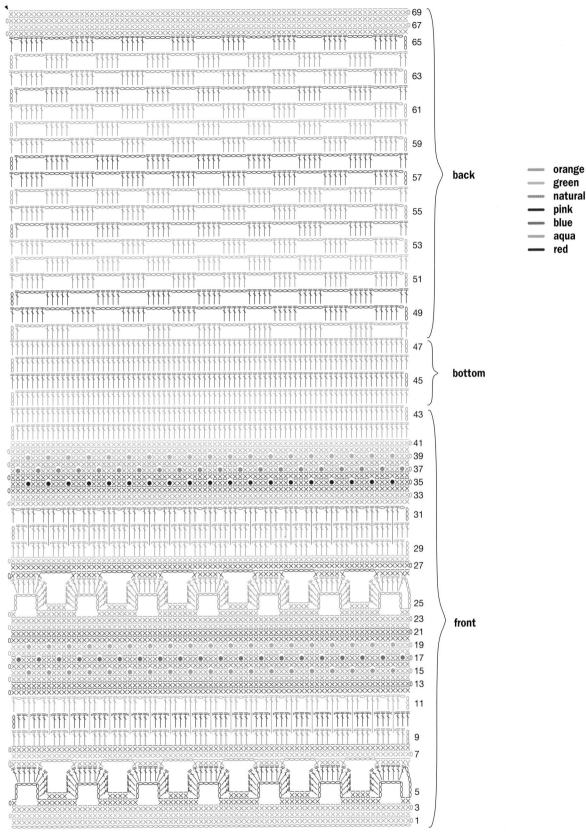

69
67
65
63
61
59
57 · back
55
53
51
49
47
45 · bottom
43
41
39
37
35
33
31
29
27
25 · front
23
21
19
17
15
13
11
9
7
5
3
1

Top Edge of Bag

$\overline{\mathsf{T}}$ dc tbl: work a double crochet, inserting the hook under only the back loop of the stitch of the previous row

$\overline{\mathsf{X}}$ sc tbl: work a single crochet, inserting the hook under only the back loop of the stitch of the previous row

● bobble: [yo, insert the hook into the stitch and draw up a loop] 3 times in the same stitch (6 loops on hook); yarn over and draw through all 6 loops at once

───── orange
───── green
───── natural
───── pink
───── blue
───── aqua
───── red

NEON

YARN: Superfine (weight category 1) cotton yarn, 1 skein (150 yd/137 m; 1.76 oz./50 g) in pink, 2 skeins in orange.
HOOK: U.S. size J-10 (6.0 mm) crochet hook
NOTIONS: Sturdy cardboard
FINISHED MEASUREMENTS: 14 by 30 in. (36 by 76 cm)
GAUGE: Rounds 1–5 = 1½ by 2¼ in. (4 by 6 cm)

NOTE: Work with two strands of yarn held together throughout the pattern.

PATTERN

With orange, ch 9. **Round 1:** Sc tbl in second ch from hook and next 7 chs, ch 1; working along the other side of the chain in the unworked loops, sc tbl in next 8 chs, ch 1, sl st in beg sc to join round. **Rounds 2–22:** Ch 1, *sc tbl in each st around to ch-sp, [sc, ch 1, sc] in ch-sp; rep from * once; sl st in beg ch to join. **Rounds 23–28:** Ch 1, sc tbl in next 104 sts, sl st in beg ch to join. **Rounds 29–42:** Continue the work as indicated in the chart. Work Rounds 29–32, Rounds 34–35, and Rounds 37–40 in pink. Fasten off.

STRAP

Row 1: Join orange in top edge where indicated in the chart. Ch 1, sc tbl in next 24 sts. Turn. **Rows 2–16:** Ch 1, sc across to last st of prev row; leave last st unworked. Turn—8 sts at the end of Row 16. **Rows 17–18:** Ch 1, sc in next 8 sts. Turn. Join pink. **Rows 19–38:** With pink, ch 1, sc in next 8 sts. Turn. Break off pink and join orange. **Rows 39–82:** Continue the work

as indicated in the chart. **Row 83:** Align the stitches of Row 82 with the stitches on the top edge of the bag opposite the base of the strap. With right sides together, work a row of sl st across the stitches of Row 82 and the top edge of the bag to attach the strap to the purse. Fasten off.

FINISHING

Cut a 4 in. (10 cm) square from the sturdy cardboard. Wrap the pink yarn around the cardboard 50 times. Tie a piece of yarn around the wraps at one edge of the cardboard, then cut through all the wraps of yarn at the other end.

Holding the bundle of yarn with the tie at the top and all the wraps hanging downward from it, wrap a length of pink yarn around the bundle a little ways from the top to form a tassel. Trim the ends of the tassel and attach it to the bottom of the bag.

14 in. (36 cm)

30 in. (76 cm)

attach to Row 42 of the purse
(along the stitches marked with
the star) with a row of sl st

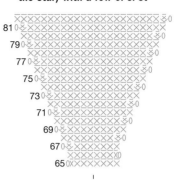

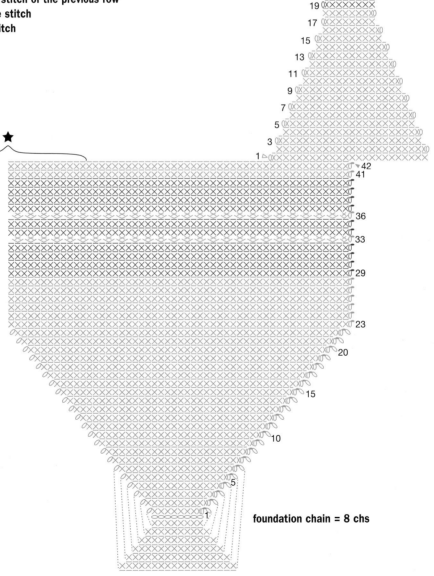

x̄ **sc tbl:** work a single crochet, inserting the hook under
only the back loop of the stitch of the previous row

work 2 sc tbl in the same stitch

work 2 sc in the same stitch

foundation chain = 8 chs

BAHAMAS

BAHAMAS

YARN: Superfine (weight category 1) cotton yarn, 8 skeins (each 150 yd/137 m; 1.76 oz./50 g) in black

HOOK: U.S. size D-3 (3.25 mm) crochet hook

NOTIONS: 18 round wooden beads, ⅛ in. (3 mm) in diameter; 1 oval wooden bead; 4 plastic rings, 1½ in. (4 cm) in diameter; sturdy cardboard, 6 by 10 in. (15 by 25 cm); black fabric for the lining; black sewing thread

FINISHED MEASUREMENTS: See schematic below

GAUGE: 17 dc and 9 rows = 4 by 4 in. (10 by 10 cm)

NOTE: Work with two strands of yarn held together throughout the pattern.

PATTERN

Ch 34. **Row 1:** Ch 3 (counts as first dc), dc in 4th ch from hook and in each ch across. **Rows 2–26:** Ch 3 (counts as first dc); dc in second st from hook and in each st across—34 sts. **Round 27:** Ch 3, dc in each st across; continue around the side, bottom edge, and opposite side of the rectangle, working 175 sts evenly around the piece; join with a sl st in top of beg ch-3. **Round 28:** Ch 3, dc in each st around, join with a sl st in top of beg ch-3. **Round 29:** Sl st in first 2 sts, ch 3, [work 4 crossed dc] 44 times, join with a sl st in top of beg ch-3. **Rounds 30–41:** Repeat Rounds 27–29. Fasten off.

EDGING AND FLAP

Round 1: Thread the 18 wooden beads onto the yarn, then attach the yarn where indicated in the stitch chart (white triangle). Ch 1, sc in next 40 sts, then make a pleat over the next 22 sts as follows: Fold the next 22 sts of the bag in two and then, working through both layers of fabric, sc in the first and 22nd sts at the same time, sc in the 2nd and 21st sts at the same time, continue in this pattern to the end of the folded section (sts in red in the stitch chart). Sc in next 4 sts, make another pleat as before, sc in next 40 sts, make another pleat, sc in next 4 sts, make another pleat, join with a sl st in beg ch—132 sts. **Rounds 2–8:** Ch 1, sc in next 132 sts, join with a sl st in beg ch. **Row 9:** Slide a bead up the yarn to the beginning of the row. Sc in next 40 sts. Turn. **Rows 10–26:** Slide a bead up the yarn to the beginning of the row; sc to last st, leaving last st unworked. Turn. **Row 27:** Ch 10, sl st in first sc of previous row. Turn. **Row 28:** Ch 1, sc in next 10 chs, sl st in last sc of Row 26. Fasten off.

HANDLE (MAKE 2)

Round 1: Attach the yarn to a ring, ch 1, work 45 sc through the ring; join with a sl st in beg ch. **Rows 2–51:** Ch 1, sc in next 8 sts. Turn. Fasten off at the end of Row 51.

Repeat these 51 rows on the second ring, but do not fasten off. Place the ends of the two straps together with right sides together and work a row of sl st across the ends, working through the stitches of both straps. Fasten off.

Make the second handle in the same way.

FINISHING

Sew the handles and the button to the purse with small stitches and black sewing thread. Sew a lining from black fabric. Place the rectangle of sturdy cardboard in the bottom of the purse, then place the lining inside the purse and sew it in place with small hidden stitches.

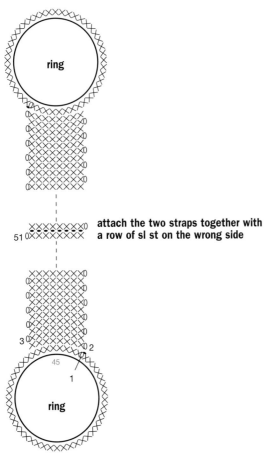

attach the two straps together with a row of sl st on the wrong side

51

3

45

1

2

Handle

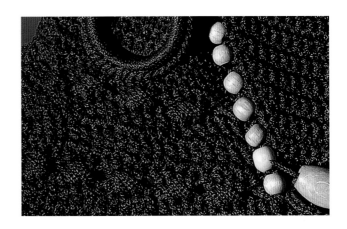

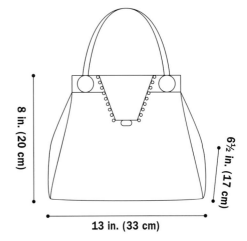

8 in. (20 cm)

6½ in. (17 cm)

13 in. (33 cm)

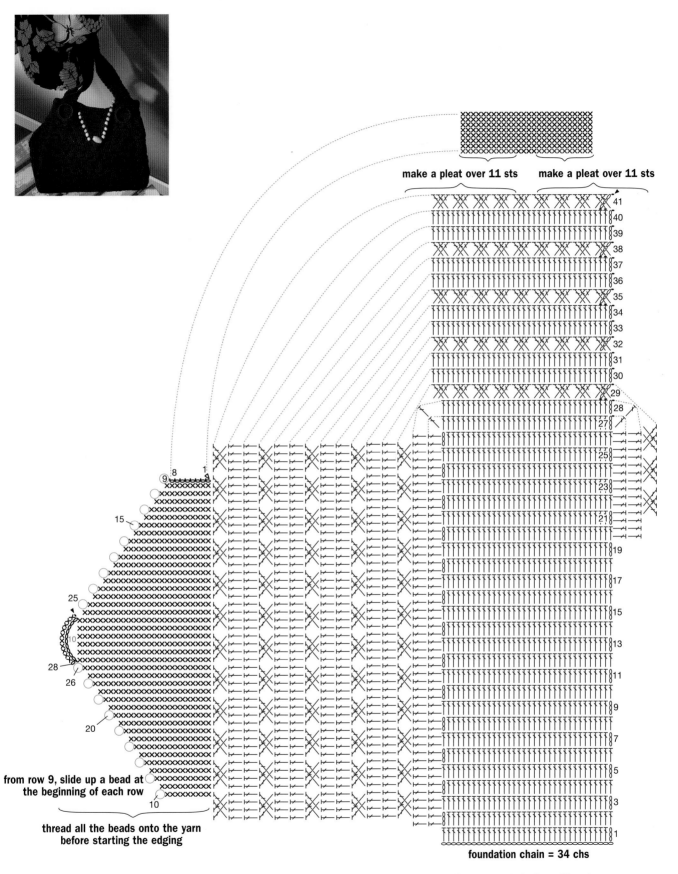

make a pleat over 11 sts   make a pleat over 11 sts

from row 9, slide up a bead at
the beginning of each row

thread all the beads onto the yarn
before starting the edging

foundation chain = 34 chs

4 crossed dc: sk next 2 sts, dc in next 2 sts; working in front of sts just made, dc in first skipped st,
dc in second skipped st

BAMBOO

YARN: Superfine (weight category 1) cotton yarn, 1 skein (150 yd/137 m; 1.76 oz./50 g) each in: pink, orange, aqua, green, light green, and blue; 2 skeins in natural
HOOK: U.S. size D-3 (3.25 mm) crochet hook
NOTIONS: 2 bamboo handles; polyester fiberfill
FINISHED MEASUREMENTS: 10½ by 11 in. (27 by 28 cm)
GAUGE: 25 sts and 17 rows in sc = 4 by 4 in. (10 by 10 cm)

PATTERN
BACK
With natural, ch 75.
Row 1: Ch 3 (counts as first dc), dc tbl in 5th ch from hook and in each ch across. Turn. **Rows 2–4:** Ch 1, sc tbl in each st across. Turn. **Row 5:** Ch 3 (counts as first dc), dc tbl in second st from hook and in each st across. Turn. **Rows 6–45:** Continue to work rows of sc tbl and dc tbl, referring to the diagram for which stitch to work each row in as well as for color order. Fasten off.

FRONT
Work as for the back.

BOBBLE (MAKE 2 IN EACH COLOR EXCEPT NATURAL)
Each bobble is worked in a continuous spiral rather than in separate rounds.

Ch 3, join with a sl st in first ch to form a ring.

Ch 1, [2 sc tbl in next st] 10 times, [sc tbl in next st] 37 times. Stop but do not fasten off. Stuff bobble with fiberfill. Pick up work again and [sc tbl in next st, sk next st] 9 times. Close top of bobble with a sl st, then work a chain of 5 to 20 sts, varying the number of chains with each ball made so they hang at different levels.

FINISHING
On the back, work a 1½ in. (4 cm) hem along the top edge of the bag. Once the hem is done, work two rows of sc tbl along the newly formed top edge with pink yarn. Do the same on the front.

Place the two pieces together with wrong sides together and assemble them by working 2 rows of sc tbl in pink through the edges of both layers of fabric around the sides and bottom of the purse. Sew the handles to the top edge. Attach one bobble in each color to the end of each handle on the front of the purse.

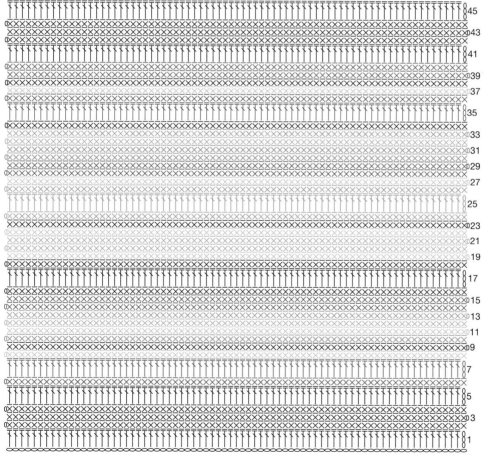

foundation chain = 75 chs

▬▬▬	pink
▬▬▬	orange
▬▬▬	aqua
▬▬▬	green
▬▬▬	light green
▬▬▬	blue
▬▬▬	natural

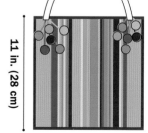

11 in. (28 cm)

10½ in. (27 cm)

‡ **dc tbl:** work a double crochet, inserting the hook under only the back loop of the stitch of the previous row

x̄ **sc tbl:** work a single crochet, inserting the hook under only the back loop of the stitch of the previous row

CARIBBEAN

YARN: Superfine (weight category 1) cotton-acrylic blend yarn, 3 skeins (each 150 yd/137 m; 1.76 oz./50 g) in blue green (with flecks of other colors)

HOOK: U.S. size D-3 (3.25 mm) crochet hook

NOTIONS: 6 packages of turquoise leather lacing; two 1¼ in. (31 mm) key rings; 2 bronze-colored keychain clips; 2 light green large heart-shaped beads; four 8 in. (20 cm) lengths of bronze-colored chain; 1 tube of clear light green seed beads; 1 tube of light green faceted beads; 4 large turquoise beads; 2 large brown beads; 2 bronze-colored leather tassels; 4 silver jump rings; 12 silver crimp beads; nylon thread

FINISHED MEASUREMENTS: 14 by 9 by 1¾ in. (36 by 23 by 4.5 cm)

GAUGE: 25 sts and 11 rows in sc = 4 by 4 in. (10 by 10 cm)

PATTERN

BAG

Ch 91.

Row 1: Ch 3 (counts as first dc), dc tbl in 5th ch from hook and in each ch across. Turn. **Rows 2–52:** Ch 3 (counts as first dc), dc tbl in second st from hook and in each st across. Turn. Mark rows 24 and 29 with small pieces of scrap yarn in a contrasting color. **Row 53:** Ch 4 (counts as first dc + 1 ch), work 3 dc in next st, skip next 3 sts, sc in next st, ch 7, skip 1 st, sc in next st, *sk next 3 sts, [3 dc, ch 3, 3 dc] in next st, sk next 3 sts, sc in next st, ch 7, sk next st, sc in next st; rep from * 7 more times, [3 dc, ch 1, dc] in last st. Turn. **Row 54:** Ch 1, sc in first st, *ch 4, sc in next ch-7 loop; rep from * to end, ch 4, sc in last st. Turn. **Rows 55–74:** Repeat Rows 53–54. Fasten off.

SIDE (MAKE 2)

Ch 11.

Row 1: Ch 3 (counts as first dc), dc tbl in 5th ch from hook and in each ch across. Turn. **Rows 2–24:** Ch 3 (counts as first dc), dc tbl in second st from hook and in each st across. Turn. Fasten off.

FINISHING

Working across the surface of the fabric, work a row of single crochet across the posts of Row 24 (one of the marked rows). Repeat on Row 29.

Attach the sides of the bag to the main piece with a row of single crochet worked through both pieces of fabric around the edge.

Strap: Cut all the leather laces in half. Take 9 of them and tie a knot at the end of each one. Insert the free end of each lace through the top edge of one of the short sides of the bag from the inside to the outside and pull it through (so that the knots end up on the inside of the bag). Thread all the laces through the two key rings, then insert them through the opposite side of the bag and knot the ends on the inside.

Clip a keychain clip on each key ring.

Hang the following charms from each keychain clip.

Charm 1: Take one of the remaining leather laces, cut it to 14 in. (35 cm), and attach a brown bead at one end and a turquoise bead at the other end. **Charm 2 (make 2 for each keychain clip):** Attach a jump ring to the end of a length of chain. Slide the jump ring onto the keychain clip. **Charm 3:** Thread a length of nylon thread through a crimp bead, then through a heart-shaped bead, then back through the crimp bead again; crimp the bead and trim the short end of the thread. Then thread 9 faceted beads and 9 turquoise seed beads onto the thread, alternating the two types of beads. Finally, pass the thread through a second crimp bead, through the end of the keychain clip, and back through the crimp bead; crimp the bead and trim the end of the thread. **Charm 4:** Thread a length of nylon thread through a crimp bead, then through the top of a tassel, then back through the crimp bead again; crimp the bead and trim the short end of the thread. Next thread on 1 turquoise seed bead, 1 faceted bead, *13 turquoise seed beads, 1 faceted bead, 1 turquoise seed bead, 1 faceted bead, 1 turquoise seed bead, 1 faceted bead; repeat the pattern from * once more, then add 13 turquoise seed beads, 1 faceted bead, 1 turquoise seed bead, and 1 crimp bead. Thread the thread back through the crimp bead, crimp the bead, and trim the end of the thread. **Charm 5:** Thread a length of nylon thread through a crimp bead, then through the 1 turquoise seed bead and 1 faceted bead, then back through the crimp bead again; crimp the bead and trim the short end of the thread. Next thread on 1 large turquoise bead, *1 faceted bead, 12 green seed beads; repeat the pattern from * 3 more times, then add 1 faceted bead and 1 crimp bead. Thread the thread back through the crimp bead, crimp the bead, and trim the end of the thread.

Cut the remaining leather laces into 6 in. (15 cm) lengths and attach them to the bottom edge of the flap.

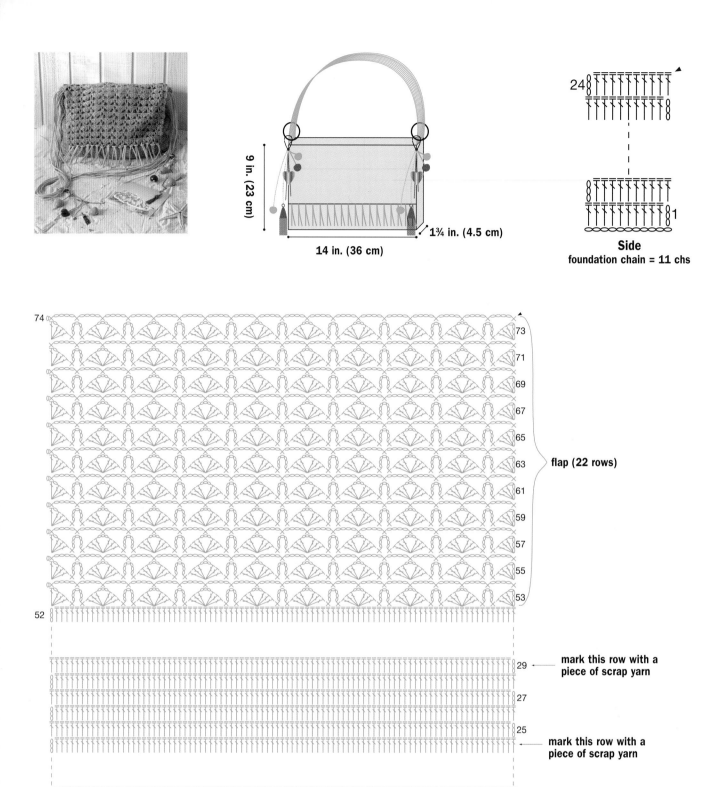

Side
foundation chain = 11 chs

9 in. (23 cm)

14 in. (36 cm)

1¾ in. (4.5 cm)

24

1

74

73

71

69

67

65

63

flap (22 rows)

61

59

57

55

53

52

29 · mark this row with a piece of scrap yarn

27

25

· mark this row with a piece of scrap yarn

1

Bag
foundation chain = 91 chs

┬ dc tbl: work a double crochet, inserting the hook under only the back loop of the stitch of the previous row

CANNES

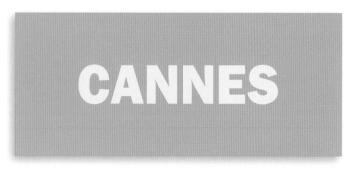

CANNES

YARN: Superfine (weight category 1) cotton-acrylic blend yarn, 1 skein (150 yd/137 m; 1.76 oz./50 g) each in gray, white, and lime green

HOOK: U.S. size D-3 (3.25 mm) crochet hook

NOTIONS: 11 silver sequins, 11 white seed beads

FINISHED MEASUREMENTS: Head circumference: 22 in. (56 cm)

GAUGE: 1 triangle motif = 2 in. (5 cm)

PATTERN

TRIANGLE MOTIF (MAKE 3)

Start with a magic loop in white.

Round 1: Ch 3 (counts as first dc), dc in ring, ch 2, [2 dc in ring, ch 2] 5 times, sl st in 3rd ch of beg ch-3 to join round. Fasten off.

Round 2: Join gray in any ch-2 sp, ch 1, sc in same ch-sp as joining, ch 8, sc in next ch-sp, [ch 4, sc in next ch-sp, ch 8, sc in next ch-sp] twice, ch 2, hdc in beg ch. **Round 3:** Ch 1, sc in same ch-sp; *[5 dc, ch 3, 5 dc] in next ch-8 sp, sc in next ch-4 sp, rep from * once more, [5 dc, ch 3, 5 dc] in final ch-8 sp, join with sl st in beg sc. Fasten off.

HAT

Round 1: Join white at the point of any triangle motif as indicated in the chart. Ch 1, sc tbl around all 3 triangles as shown in the diagram. Join with a sl st in beg ch. **Round 2:** Ch 1, sc tbl in next 13 sts, ch 20, [sc tbl in next 15 sts, ch 20] twice, sc tbl in next 2 sts, join with a sl st in beg ch.

Rounds 3–13: Continue as indicated in the chart. Work Rounds 3, 5, 6, and 9–13 in gray, Rounds 4 and 8 in white, and Round 7 in lime green.

FLOWER (MAKE 8)

With lime green, ch 5, then join with a sl st to form a ring. [Ch 4, sl st in ring] 5 times. Fasten off.

FINISHING

Sew one seed bead and one sequin to the center of each triangle. Sew a seed bead and a sequin to the center of each flower. Sew the flowers around the bottom edge of the hat. Weave in all ends.

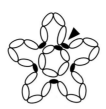

Flower
make 8 in lime green

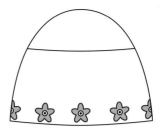

head circumference: 22 in. (56 cm)

dc tbl: work a double crochet, inserting the hook under only the back loop of the stitch of the previous row

sc tbl: work a single crochet, inserting the hook under only the back loop of the stitch of the previous row

work 2 sc in same stitch

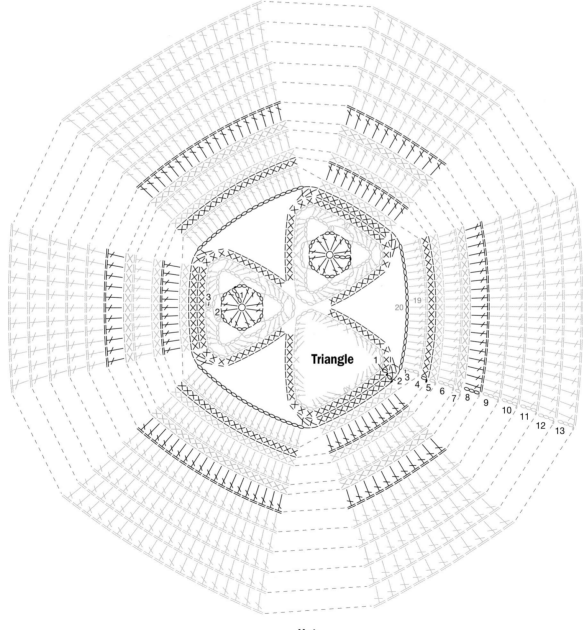

Hat

BRICKWORK PURSE AND NECKLACE

BRICKWORK PURSE AND NECKLACE

YARN: Superfine (weight category 1) cotton-acrylic blend yarn, 1 skein (150 yd/137 m; 1.76 oz./50 g) each in: red-orange, lime green, beige, and natural
HOOK: U.S. size D-3 (3.25 mm) crochet hook
NOTIONS: 4 green mother-of-pearl buttons, 1 in. (2.5 cm) in diameter
FINISHED MEASUREMENTS: 13 by 9 in. (33 by 23 cm); 1 in. (2.5 cm) deep
GAUGE: Motif A = 4¼ by 2¼ in. (11 by 6 cm)

PATTERN

Make 2 of each of the following motifs:
Motif A: With lime green, chain 17. **Row 1:** Sc tbl in second ch from hook and in each ch across—16 sts. **Rows 2–23:** Ch 1, turn. Sc tbl in each st across. Fasten off. **Motif B:** With red-orange, chain 22. **Row 1:** Sc tbl in second ch from hook and in each ch across—21 sts. **Rows 2–13:** Ch 1, turn. Sc tbl in each st across. Fasten off. **Motif C:** With beige, chain 17.

Row 1: Sc tbl in second ch from hook and in each ch across—16 sts. **Rows 2–13:** Ch 1, turn. Sc tbl in each st across. Fasten off. **Motif D:** With lime green, chain 7. **Row 1:** Sc tbl in second ch from hook and in each ch across—6 sts. **Rows 2–13:** Ch 1, turn. Sc tbl in each st across. Fasten off. **Motif E:** With red-orange, chain 16. **Row 1:** Sc tbl in second ch from hook and in each ch across—15 sts. **Rows 2–7:** Ch 1, turn. Sc tbl in each st across. Fasten off. **Motif F:** With beige, chain 13. **Row 1:** Sc tbl in second ch from hook and in each ch across—12 sts. **Rows 2–10:** Ch 1, turn. Sc tbl in each st across. Fasten off. **Motif G:** With lime green, chain 17. **Row 1:** Sc tbl in second ch from hook and in each ch across—16 sts. **Rows 2–10:** Ch 1, turn. Sc tbl in each st across. Fasten off. **Motif H:** With red-orange, chain 16. **Row 1:** Sc tbl in second ch from hook and in each ch across—15 sts. **Rows 2–14:** Ch 1, turn. Sc tbl in each st across. Fasten off. **Motif I:** With beige, chain 9. **Row 1:** Sc tbl in second ch from hook and in each ch across—8 sts. **Rows 2–20:** Ch 1, turn. Sc tbl in each st across. Fasten off. **Motif J:** With lime green, chain 8. **Row 1:** Sc tbl in second ch from hook and in each ch across—7 sts. **Rows 2–20:** Ch 1, turn. Sc tbl in each st across. Fasten off. **Motif K:** With beige, chain 17. **Row 1:** Sc tbl in second ch from hook and in each ch across—16 sts. **Rows 2–19:** Ch 1, turn. Sc tbl in each st across. Fasten off. **Motif L:** With red-orange, chain 17. **Row 1:** Sc tbl in second ch from hook and in each ch across—16 sts. **Rows 2–19:** Ch 1, turn. Sc tbl in each st across. Fasten off. **Motif M:** With beige, chain 13. **Row 1:** Sc tbl in second ch from hook and in each ch across—12 sts. **Rows 2–19:** Ch 1, turn. Sc tbl in each st across. Fasten off. **Motif N:** With lime green, chain 20. **Row 1:** Sc tbl in second ch from hook and in each ch across—19 sts. **Rows 2–15:** Ch 1, turn. Sc tbl in each st across. Fasten off. **Motif O:** With red-orange, chain 12. **Row 1:** Sc tbl in second ch from hook and in each ch across—11 sts. **Rows 2–15:** Ch 1, turn. Sc tbl in each st across. Fasten off.

FINISHING

Back: With the natural yarn, assemble the motifs as shown in the diagram below by working a row of single crochet through both motifs along each join. **Front:** Make identical to the back.

SIDE

With natural, chain 161.
Row 1: Sc in second ch from hook and in each ch across—160 sts. **Row 2:** Ch 1, turn. *Sc tbl in next 2 sts, bobble in next st; rep from * to last 2 sts, sc tbl in last 2 sts. **Row 3:** Ch 1, turn. Sc tbl in each st across. Fasten off. Attach the side piece to the front and back with a row of single crochet in natural yarn through both pieces along the whole edge. Join natural anywhere on top edge of purse and crochet a row of single crochet all the way around the top opening.

HANDLE (MAKE 2)

With natural, chain 91.
Row 1: Sc in second ch from hook and in each ch across—90 sts. **Row 2:** Ch 1, turn. *Sc tbl in next 2 sts, bobble in next st; rep from * to last 2 sts, sc tbl in last 2 sts. **Rows 3–5:** Ch 1, turn. Sc tbl in each st across. Fasten off. **Row 6:** Fold handle in half so that Row 5 and the foundation chain are lined up. Ch 1, sc in next 90 sts, working through the sts of Row 5 and the unworked loops of the foundation chain at the same time. Fasten off. Sew the ends of the handles to the outside of the bag, about 2¼ in. (6 cm) from the edge. Sew a button to each end of each handle.

■ red-orange

□ lime green

▨ beige

x̄ **sc tbl:** work a single crochet, inserting the hook under only the back loop of the stitch of the previous row

● **bobble:** [yo, insert hook into stitch, yo, pull up a loop] 3 times, yo, pull through all 7 loops

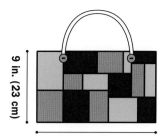

9 in. (23 cm)

13 in. (33 cm)
Back and Front

fold the handle in half and work
Row 6 through Row 5 and
foundation chain at same time

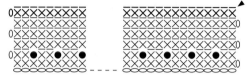

Handle
foundation chain = 90 chs
make 2 in natural

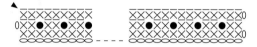

Side
foundation chain = 160 chs
make 2 in natural

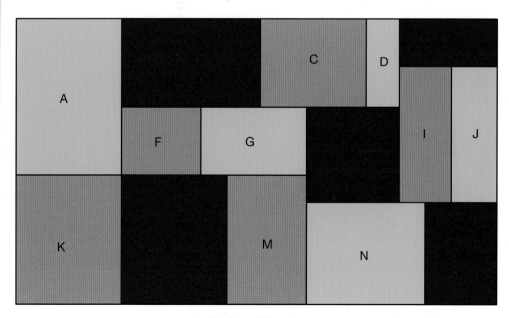

Back and Front

YARN: Superfine (weight category 1) cotton-acrylic blend yarn, 1 skein (150 yd/137 m; 1.76 oz./50 g) each in: natural, lime green, and light green

HOOK: U.S. size C-2 (2.75 mm) crochet hook

NOTIONS: 1 tube of large grass-green seed beads; 24 wooden disks, ⅜ in. (1 cm) in diameter; beads in the following colors: 3 black, 3 khaki, 3 brown; 1 packet of copper-colored chains; 12 silver crimp beads; 12 silver jump rings; 9 wooden beads, ¾ in. (2 cm) in diameter; nylon thread

FINISHED MEASUREMENTS: see schematic below

GAUGE: 1 sphere = ½ in. (1.3 cm)

PATTERN
SPHERE (MAKE 3 IN EACH COLOR)

Ch 4, join with a sl st to form a ring. Work in a spiral as follows: Ch 1, [2 sc in next st] 12 times, [sc in next st] 50 times, insert a wooden bead into the piece, [sk next st, sc in next st] 12 times. Fasten off, leaving a tail a few inches long. Thread the tail through the remaining stitches, pull tight, and fasten off, hiding the end of the tail inside the sphere.

ASSEMBLY

Thread a crimp bead and a jump ring onto a length of nylon thread, then bring the thread back through the crimp bead and crimp the bead firmly with a pair of pliers to hold the thread in place. Thread the following sequence of beads onto the thread: 1 seed bead, 1 wooden disk, 1 green seed beed, 1 sphere in lime green, 1 seed bead, 1 wooden disk, 1 seed bead, 1 black bead, 1 seed bead, 1 wooden disk, 1 seed bead, 1 light green sphere, 1 seed bead, 1 wooden disk, 1 seed bead. Finish with a crimp bead and a jump ring, then bring the end of the thread back through the crimp bead, crimp the bead firmly, and cut off the end of the thread.

Partially open one of the jump rings and thread the ends of 2 lengths of chain 12 links long each onto it. Close the ring. Do the same with the jump ring at the other end of the thread.

Attach a jump ring to the end of another length of nylon thread using a crimp bead, as before, and thread the following sequence of beads onto the prepared thread: 1 seed bead, 1 wooden disk, 1 seed bead, 1 khaki bead, 1 seed bead, 1 wooden disk, 1 seed bead, 1 natural sphere, 1 seed bead, 1 wooden disk, 1 seed bead, 1 brown bead, 1 seed bead, 1 wooden disk, 1 seed bead. Finish the end with another crimp bead and jump ring. Open the jump rings and thread the other ends of the lengths of chain from the first set of beads into one of them, and two new lengths of chain into the other one. Close the jump rings.

Repeat the above instructions 2 more times for a total of 6 sequences of beads. Attach them all together with the chains and jump rings.

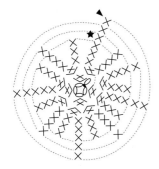

insert the wooden bead into the middle at the point marked with the black star

Sphere
make 3 in lime green, 3 in light green, and 3 in natural

⪦ **work 2 single crochet in the same stitch**

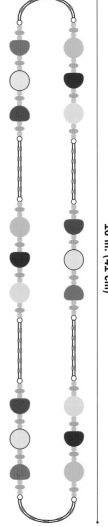

16 in. (41 cm)

ROARING TWENTIES

ROARING TWENTIES

YARN: Superfine (weight category 1) cotton yarn, 2 skeins (each 150 yd/137 m; 1.76 oz./50 g) in black
HOOK: U.S. size D-3 (3.25 mm) crochet hook
FINISHED MEASUREMENTS: Head circumference = 22 in. (56 cm)
GAUGE: Flower = 4¾ in. (12 cm) in diameter

PATTERN
HAT

Ch 5, join with a sl st to form a ring.
Round 1: Ch 1, sc tbl in each ch around; join with a sl st in beg ch. **Round 2:** Ch 1, 2 sc tbl in each st around; join with a sl st in beg ch. **Round 3:** Ch 1, sc tbl in each st around; join with a sl st in beg ch. **Rounds 4–26:** Continue as indicated in the stitch chart. Fasten off.

FLOWER

Ch 8, join with a sl st to form a ring.
Round 1: Ch 3 (counts as first dc), ch 1, [2 dc in ring, ch 1] 7 times, dc in ring; join with sl st to third ch of beg ch-3. **Round 2:** Sl st in next ch, ch 1, sc in ch-sp, [ch 5, sc in next ch-sp] 7 times, ch 2, dc in beg ch. **Round 3:** Ch 4 (counts as first tr), 2 tr around post of dc of prev rnd (as if post of dc were part of a ch-5 sp), *[3 tr, ch 9, 3 tr] in next ch-5 sp, rep from * 7 times, 3 tr in next ch-5 sp, ch 4, dtr in 4th ch of beg ch-4. **Round 4:** Ch 3 (counts as first dc), 9 dc around post of dtr of prev rnd (as if post were part of a ch-9 sp), *[10 dc, ch 3, 10 dc] in next ch-9 sp, rep from * 7 times, 10 dc in next ch-9 sp, ch3, sl st in top ch of beg ch-3. Fasten off. Sew the flower onto the hat near the brim.

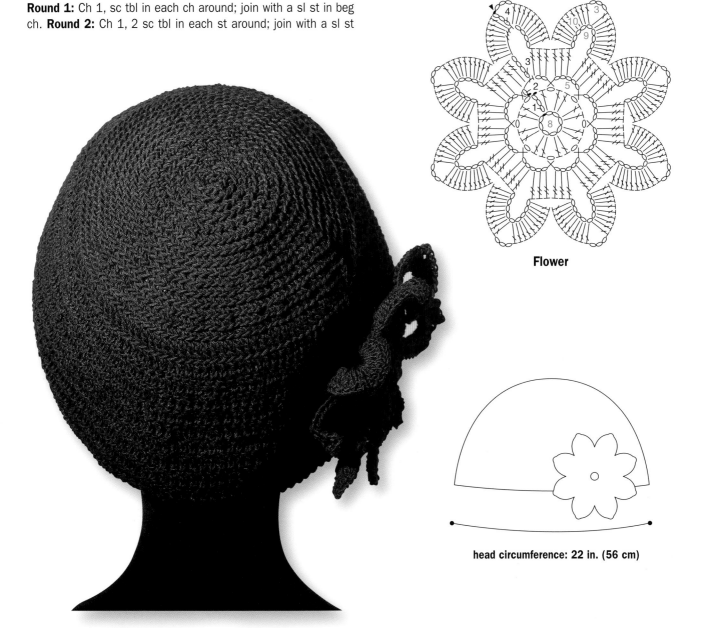

Flower

head circumference: 22 in. (56 cm)

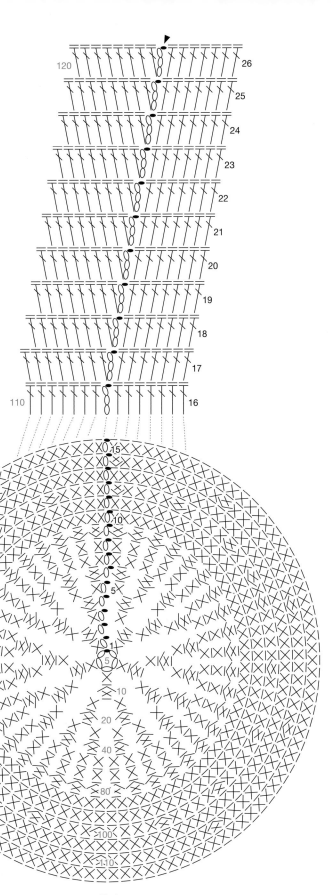

Hat

$\overline{\underset{\top}{|}}$ dc tbl: work a double crochet, inserting the hook under only the back loop of the stitch of the previous row

$\overline{\times}$ sc tbl: work a single crochet, inserting the hook under only the back loop of the stitch of the previous row

$\underset{\times}{\lessgtr}$ work 2 sc tbl in same stitch

SIXTIES

YARN: Superfine (weight category 1) cotton-acrylic blend yarn, 1 skein (150 yd/137 m; 1.76 oz./50 g) each in: light green, aqua, and white
HOOK: U.S. size D-3 (3.25 mm) crochet hook
FINISHED MEASUREMENTS: 7 by 6½ in. (17 by 18 cm)
GAUGE: 24 sts and 20 rows = 4 by 4 in. (10 by 10 cm)

PATTERN
BACK

With light green, ch 4, join with a sl st to form a ring.
Round 1: Ch 1, [sc tbl in next ch, ch 1] 4 times, join with a sl st in beg ch. **Rounds 2–17:** Ch 1, *sc tbl in each st to next ch-sp, [sc, ch 1, sc] in ch-sp; rep from * around; join with a sl st in beg ch. Fasten off. **Round 18:** Join the yarn in the top left corner (where indicated in the diagram). Ch 1, *sc tbl in each st to next ch-sp, [sc, ch 1, sc] in ch-sp; rep from * once more; sc tbl in each st to next ch-sp, sc in ch-sp; ch 250, sl st in beg ch. **Round 19:** Ch 1, *sc tbl in each st to next ch-sp, [sc, ch 1, sc] in ch-sp; rep from * once more; sc tbl in each st to next ch-sp, sc in ch-sp, sc tbl in each ch around strap, join with a sl st in beg ch. Fasten off.

FRONT
Work same as back.

ASSEMBLY
Place the two pieces together with wrong sides together and join the yarn anywhere along the edge. Work a row of sc tbl around the entire edge of both pieces except for the strap, going through both layers, (working [sc, ch 1, sc] in both bottom corners as always) to join them together. Join the halves of the strap together with a row of sc tbl worked with right sides together (in gray in the stitch chart) and continue the row around the top opening of the bag if desired.

FLOWER (MAKE 3)
With aqua, ch 5, join with a sl st to form a ring.
Round 1: Ch 1, 5 sc in ring, join with a sl st in beg ch. **Round 2:** Ch 1, [ch 3, sc in second ch from hook and in next ch, sc through central ring (working over sc of prev rnd)] 5 times, join with a sl st in beg ch. Fasten off.

LEAF (MAKE 6)
With white, ch 4.
Work in a spiral as follows: Sc in second ch from hook and in next 2 chs, ch 1, working in the unused loops of the foundation ch work 4 sc, ch 1, continuing around to work in the first sts made work 4 sc. Fasten off.

FINISHING
Sew the flowers and leaves to the bag as shown in the illustration below.

Flower
make 3 in aqua

Ⓧ **sc through the center ring**

Leaf
(make 6 in white)
foundation chain = 3 chs

strap (250 sts)

assemble the purse front and back with a row of sc tbl

assemble the strap front and back with a row of sc tbl

19
18

Back and Front
make 2 in green

x **sc tbl: work a single crochet, inserting the hook under only the back loop of the stitch of the previous row**

7 in. (18 cm)

6½ in. (17 cm)

VALENTINE

YARN: Superfine (weight category 1) cotton-acrylic blend yarn, 1 skein (150 yd/137 m; 1.76 oz./50 g) each in: light pink and dark pink

HOOK: U.S. size D-3 (3.25 mm) crochet hook

NOTIONS: Two half-circle rings for attatching the strap; 2 pink wooden beads, ¾ in. (18 mm) in diameter; 1½ yd. (1.4 m) pink ribon, ¼ in. (6 mm) wide

FINISHED MEASUREMENTS: 6 by 6¼ in. (15 by 16 cm)

GAUGE: 24 sts and 20 rows = 4 by 4 in. (10 by 10 cm)

PATTERN

BACK

With light pink, ch 40.

Row 1: Sc in second ch from hook and in each ch across. Turn.
Rows 2–31: Ch 1, sc tbl in each st across. Turn. **Rows 32–35:** Ch 1, sc tbl in next 5 sts. Turn. **Row 36:** Thread the tab through a half-circle ring, then fold it down. Attach the tab in place with a final row of 5 sc tbl, inserting the hook through the sts of Rows 32 and 35 at the same time for each st. Fasten off.

FRONT

Work as for the back, but work the stitches indicated in the diagram below in dark pink.

FINISHING

Place the two pieces together with wrong sides together and work a row of single crochet around the sides and bottom of the pieces to join them together.

Thread a wooden bead onto one end of the ribbon, then thread the ribbon through one of the rings; fold the end back on itself and sew firmly, then pull the bead down to cover the stitches. Repeat on the other side.

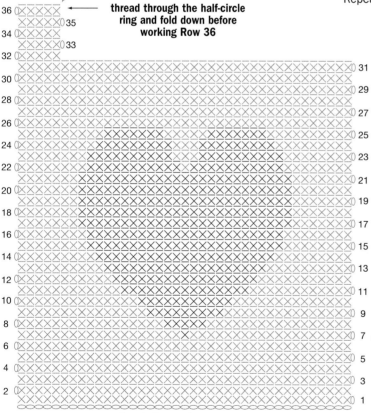

thread through the half-circle ring and fold down before working Row 36

foundation chain = 39 chs
Front: light pink and medium pink
Back: solid light pink

x̄ **sc tbl: work a single crochet, inserting the hook under only the back loop of the stitch of the previous row**

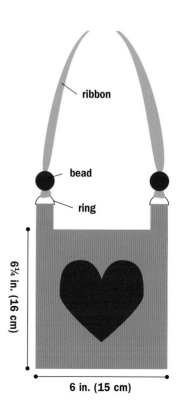

ribbon

bead

ring

6¼ in. (16 cm)

6 in. (15 cm)

INVITATION

YARN: Superfine (weight category 1) cotton yarn, 8 skeins (each 150 yd/137 m; 1.76 oz./50 g) in black, 2 skeins in ivory
HOOK: U.S. size G-6 (4.0 mm) crochet hook
NOTIONS: 2 semicircular bamboo handles; 36 small gold beads
FINISHED MEASUREMENTS: 12 by 13 in. (30 by 33 in.)
GAUGE: 22 sts and 15 rows = 4 by 4 in. (10 by 10 cm)

PATTERN
BAG
Working with 2 strands of black held together as one, ch 71.
Row 1: Sc in second ch from hook and in each ch across. Turn.
Row 2: Ch 3 (counts as first dc), sk first st, dc in each st across. Turn. **Row 3:** Ch 1, sc in each st across. Turn.

Repeat Rows 2–3 until piece measures 13 in. (33 cm) tall. Fasten off.

Make another piece just like the first.

FLOWER (MAKE 36)
With 2 strands of ivory held together as one, ch 8, join with a sl st to form a ring.
Round 1: Ch 3 (counts as first dc), 17 dc in ring, join with sl st in 3rd ch of beg ch-3. Fasten off.

FINISHING
Sew the two parts of the bag together along the sides and bottom, leaving the top 4 in. (10 cm) open on each side.

Fold under the top 1 in. (2.5 cm) of each top edge over the straight side of a handle and sew in place.

Sew the flowers to the bag with the gold beads in the middle as shown in the illustration below.

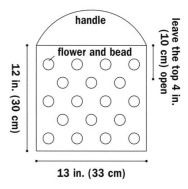

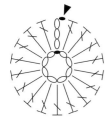

Flower
make 36 in ivory

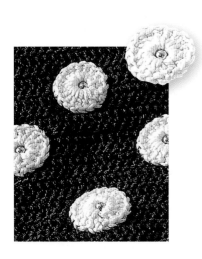

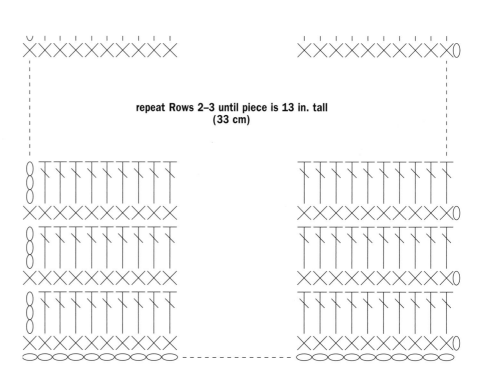

repeat Rows 2–3 until piece is 13 in. tall (33 cm)

foundation chain = 70 chs

THE BIG DAY

YARN: Superfine (weight category 1) cotton yarn, 2 skeins (each 150 yd/137 m; 1.76 oz./50 g) in white, 1 skein in light blue
HOOK: U.S. size D-3 (3.25 mm) crochet hook
FINISHED MEASUREMENTS: see schematic below
GAUGE: 24 sts and 13 rows = 4 by 4 in. (10 by 10 cm)

PATTERN

FRONT AND BACK
With white, ch 58.
Row 1: Dc in fourth ch from hook and in each ch across. **Rows 2–62:** Ch 3, turn. Dc in second st from hook and in each st across. Fasten off.

SIDE (MAKE 2)
With white, ch 11.
Row 1: Dc in fourth ch from hook and in each ch across. **Rows 2–19:** Ch 3, turn. Dc in second st from hook and in each st across. Fasten off.

ASSEMBLY
Attach the side pieces to the main piece that forms the front, back, and bottom of the bag with a row of sl st around the three sides of each side piece: First line up and attach the 19 rows of the front with one side of the side piece, then attach the bottom edge of the side to the next 4 rows of the main piece, and finally attach the next 19 rows of both pieces, leaving the last 20 rows of the main piece free for a flap. Repeat on the other side.

STRAP
Row 1: Join white at the top edge of one of the side pieces, ch 1, sc in next st, [ch 3, 2 dc in third ch from hook] twice, sc in last stitch of side piece. **Row 2:** Ch 4, turn. Work 3 dc in each ch-3 arc of prev row, tr in sc of prev row. **Row 3:** Ch 1, turn. Sc in next tr, [ch 3, 2 dc in third ch from hook] twice, sc in top of ch-4 of prev row. **Rows 4–54:** Repeat Rows 2–3. **Row 55:** Line up the end of the strap with the side piece on the opposite side of the bag. Working through the sts of both pieces at the same time, sl st in each st across end of strap and top edge of side piece.

FLOWERS (MAKE 3)
With blue, ch 8; join with a sl st to form a ring.
Round 1: Ch 1, 12 sc in ring, join with a sl st in beg ch. **Round 2:** Ch 1, *sc in next st, ch 3, sk next st; rep from * around; join with a sl st in beg ch. **Round 3:** Sl st in next sc and in next ch-3 arc. Ch 1, [sc, 5 dc, sc] in each ch-3 arc around; join with a sl st in beg ch. Fasten off.

Sew the flowers to the bottom right corner of the flap with small stitches. Weave in all ends.

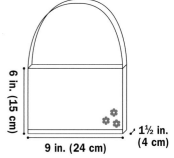

6 in. (15 cm)

9 in. (24 cm)

1½ in. (4 cm)

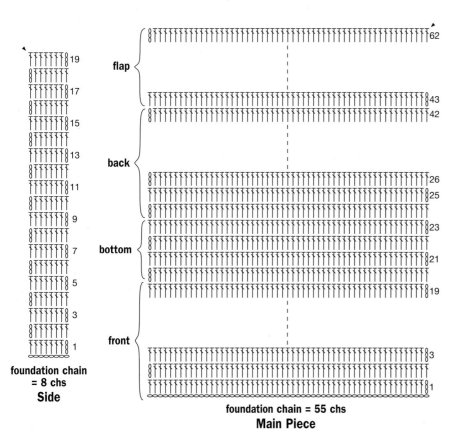

foundation chain = 8 chs
Side

flap
back
bottom
front

foundation chain = 55 chs
Main Piece

62
43
42
26
25
23
21
19
3
1

19
17
15
13
11
9
7
5
3
1

attach to the other side of the bag with sl st

54
53

2
1

join the yarn at the top edge of either side piece
Strap

3
2
1

Flower
(make 3 in blue)

SLAVIC PURSE
AND ACCESSORIES

SLAVIC PURSE AND ACCESSORIES

Row 1: Sc tbl in second ch from hook and in each ch across. **Row 2 (repeat this row for mesh stitch):** Ch 2, turn. *Sk next st, sc tbl in next st, ch 1; rep from * to end of row, ending with 1 sc in last st. Repeat Row 2 until piece measures 8 in. (20 cm).

HANDLE SECTION

Rows 1–5: Ch 1, turn. Sc in each st across. **Rows 6–9:** Ch 1, turn. Sc in next 10 sts. Set aside but do not fasten off. Join two more strands of yarn with a sl st where indicated in the diagram and repeat Rows 6–9 on the other side of the piece. At the end of Row 9, ch 18 and join to other side of gap with a sl st. Fasten off and take up work again at end of first Row 9. **Rows 10–26:** Continue as indicated in the diagram, working 8 more rows of straight single crochet, then repeating rows 6–9 to form another rectangular gap, and finishing with 5 more rows of straight crochet.

FRONT

Work same as back.

FINISHING

Fold down top portion of the back piece. Work a round of sc all the way around the inside edge of the hand hole with smaller hook and two strands of yarn, working through both layers of fabric; join the end of the round to the beginning with a sl st and fasten off.

Work a row of single crochet along one edge of the handle section, with two strands of yarn and working through both layers of fabric. Slide a dowel into the top portion of the handle section and close up the other side seam with another row of single crochet.

Finish the front piece in the same way.

Attach the front and back together with a row of sc tbl around the sides and bottom.

YARN: Superfine (weight category 1) cotton yarn, 4 skeins (each 150 yd/137 m; 1.76 oz./50 g) in black

HOOKS: U.S. size G-6 (4.0 mm) and H-8 (5.0 mm) crochet hooks

NOTIONS: Two 9-in. (23-cm) wooden dowels, ⅜ in. (1 cm) in diameter

FINISHED MEASUREMENTS: 10 by 12 in. (25 by 30 cm)

GAUGE: 16 sts and 14 rows in mesh stitch = 4 by 4 in. (10 by 10 cm)

PATTERN
BACK

With two strands of yarn and larger hook, chain 37.

Handle Section

fold here

26
24
22
20
18
16
14
12
10
08
06
04
02

20
18

8
6

work 8 in. (20 cm) in mesh stitch

5

3

01

foundation chain = 36 chs
Front and Back

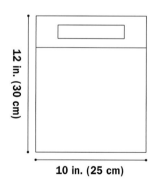

12 in. (30 cm)

10 in. (25 cm)

x̄ **sc tbl:** work a single crochet, inserting the hook under only the back loop of the stitch of the previous row

YARN: Superfine (weight category 1) cotton yarn, 1 skein (150 yd/137 m; 1.76 oz./50 g) in black

HOOK: U.S. size D-3 (3.25 mm) crochet hook

NOTIONS: 1 zipper, 4¾ in. (12 cm) long; 3 iridescent sequins; 3 black beads

FINISHED MEASUREMENTS: 4 by 3 in. (10 by 7.5 cm)

PATTERN

Ch 8.

Round 1: Sc tbl in second ch from hook and in each ch across; sc tbl again in end ch to go around end to other side of chain; sc tbl in unused loops of each ch across other side of ch, join with sl st in turning ch. **Rounds 2–4:** Ch 1, *sc tbl in next st, 2 sc tbl in next st; rep from * around, join with sl st in beg ch. **Rounds 5–12:** Continue as indicated in the diagram. Fasten off.

FLOWER

Ch 3, join with sl st to form a ring.

Round 1: Ch 1, [sc in ring, ch 3] 5 times, join with sl st in beg ch. Ch 5 for the stem, then fasten off. Make 2 more flowers, one with a stem of 10 chs, and 1 with a stem of 15 chs.

FINISHING

Sew the zipper in the top opening of the coin purse. Sew a bead and a sequin in the center of each flower.

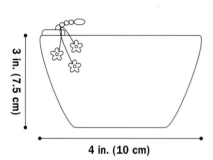

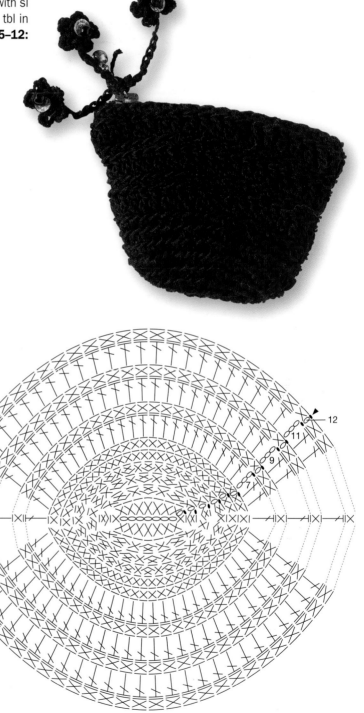

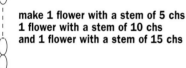

make 1 flower with a stem of 5 chs
1 flower with a stem of 10 chs
and 1 flower with a stem of 15 chs

Flower

 dc tbl: work a double crochet, inserting the hook under only the back loop of the stitch of the previous row

⨉ **sc tbl:** work a single crochet, inserting the hook under only the back loop of the stitch of the previous row

❀ **work 2 sc tbl in the same stitch**

foundation chain = 7 chs

YARN: Superfine (weight category 1) cotton yarn, small amounts in: white, orange, red, magenta, and lime green

HOOK: U.S. size D-3 (3.25 mm) crochet hook

NOTIONS: 1 tube of yellow seed beads; 13 red sequins; 13 red seed beads; 2 purple sequins for the eyes; 2 black seed beads; black and red thread or embroidery floss; 1 pin back

FINISHED MEASUREMENTS: 3½ by 2 in. (9 by 5 cm)

PATTERN

With magenta, chain 5.

Row 1: Sc tbl in second ch from hook and in each ch across—4 sc. Ch 1. Turn. **Row 2:** Ch 1, sc tbl in last ch of prev row and in each st across, ch 1—5 sc. Turn. **Row 3:** Ch 1, sc tbl in last ch of prev row and in each st across, ch 1—6 sc. Turn. **Rows 4–12:** Continue in sc tbl, changing colors and increasing and decreasing as indicated in the diagram. **Round 13:** With green, ch 1, sc tbl in next 5 sts, ch 18, sl st in beg ch. **Round 14:** With white, ch 1, work 21 sc evenly spaced around ring, join with a sl st in beg ch. **Round 15:** Ch 1, *sc tbl in next st, sk next st; rep from * around. Do not join at end of round but continue in a spiral in the same stitch pattern until the center of the face is filled in. Fasten off.

Border: Join red at the bottom left corner. Ch 1. Sc tbl around the entire piece, working in row ends and in unused loops of chain around head. Skip the row ends at the neck and add or omit additional stitches as needed to achieve an even border around the piece.

FINISHING

Sew the purple sequins to the face for eyes with the black seed beads in the middle. Embroider eyelashes around the eyes with black thread. Embroider the mouth with red thread. Sew the red sequins around the face with a red seed bead in the center of each one. Sew the yellow seed beads around the outer edge of the piece. Finally, sew the pin back to the back of the piece.

continue in a spiral in white, single crocheting in every other stitch

x̄ **sc tbl: work a single crochet, inserting the hook under only the back loop of the stitch of the previous row**

border

15
14
13
12
11
9
7
5
3
1

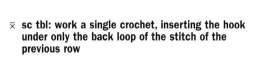

YARN: Superfine (weight category 1) cotton-acrylic blend yarn, 1 skein (150 yd/137 m; 1.76 oz./50 g) each in: fuchsia, red, and light green

HOOK: U.S. size C-2 (2.75 mm) crochet hook

NOTIONS: 2 iridescent green buttons, 5/8 in. (15 mm) in diameter; 2 pin backs

FINISHED MEASUREMENTS: 2¾ in. (6 cm)

PATTERN

FLOWER A (MAKE 2)

With fuchsia, *ch 2, [2 dc, 3 tr, ch 3, sl st] in second ch from hook (1 petal formed). Rep from * 2 more times. Join to base of first petal with a sl st. Fasten off.

FLOWER B (MAKE 2)

With red, ch 7, join with a sl st to form a ring.

Round 1: Ch 1, 10 sc in ring, join with sl st in beg ch. **Round 2:** Ch 1, [sc in next st, sk next st, ch 3] 5 times, sl st in beg ch.

Round 3: *[Dc, tr, dtr, trtr, dtr, tr, dc, sl st] in next ch-3 sp; rep from * around, placing final sl st in same ch as final sl st of Round 2. Fasten off.

LEAF BASE (MAKE 2)

With light green, [ch 15, sc in second ch from hook and in next 13 chs] 5 times, sl st in base of first ch. Fasten off.

FINISHING

Stack a Flower A, a Flower B, and a Leaf Base together in that order. Place a button on the top center and sew the whole stack together through the button with green yarn. Sew the pin back to the back of the piece.

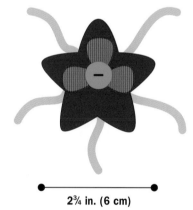

2¾ in. (6 cm)

Flower A
(make 2 in fuchsia)

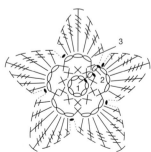

Flower B
(make 2 in red)

Leaf Base
(make 2 in light green)

YARN: Superfine (weight category 1) cotton-acrylic blend yarn, scrap amounts of light green and peach

HOOK: Any size crochet hook

NOTIONS: Kilt pin with 3 rings for attachments; 1 package of copper-colored chains; 3 gold jump rings; 9 large green seed beads; sewing thread to match the yarn colors

FINISHED MEASUREMENTS: 1 flower = ¾ in. (2 cm) in diameter

PATTERN

Ch 5, join with a sl st to form a ring.

Round 1: [Ch 4, sl st in ring] 5 times. Fasten off.

Make 5 flowers in green and 4 in peach.

FINISHING

Sew a bead in the center of each flower. Prepare 9 chains of different lengths (6, 13, 26, 8, 29, 18, 18, 14, and 5 links). Attach 3 chains to each jump ring, then sew the flowers to the ends of the chains so that two groups have 2 green flowers and 1 peach one and the other group has 1 green flower and 2 peach ones. Attach the jump rings to the rings in the kilt pin, with the ring with the 2 peach flowers in the middle.

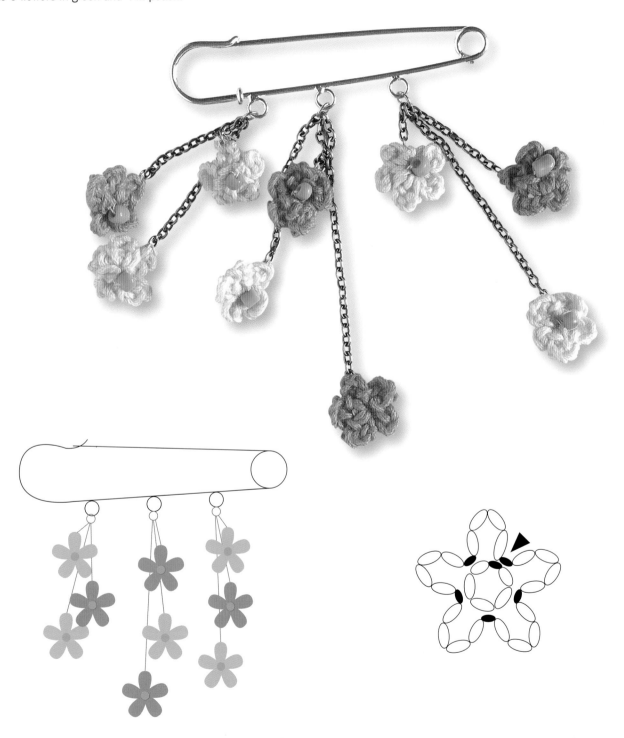

TAHITI

TAHITI

YARN: Superfine (weight category 1) cotton yarn, 1 skein (150 yd/137 m; 1.76 oz./50 g) each in: orange, green, and yellow
HOOK: U.S. size 8 (1.5 mm) steel hook
NOTIONS: 1 pair of plastic flip-flops, 2 clear faceted beads, fabric glue (optional)

PATTERN
FLOWER (MAKE 2)
With orange, make a magic loop.
Round 1: Ch 1, work 10 sc in loop, pull end of yarn to tighten loop, join with a sl st in beg sc. **Round 2:** Ch 1, *sc in next st, ch 3, sk next st; rep from * 4 more times, join with a sl st in beg ch. **Round 3:** Sl st in next st and in ch-3 arc, ch 1, [sc, 4 dc, sc] in each ch-3 arc around. Join with a sl st in first ch. **Rounds 4–7:** Continue as indicated in the stitch chart. Start Rounds 5 and 7 by working in sl st to get to the next ch arc. Fasten off.

LEAF (MAKE 4)
With green, ch 13, dc in 4th ch from hook and in next 7 chs, in last ch work [2 sc, ch 1, 2 sc]. Continue in unused loops on other side of ch, working 1 dc in each ch to end. Fasten off.

FINISHING
Wrap the straps of each flip-flop with yellow yarn. Sew or glue 1 flower, 2 leaves, and 1 faceted bead to the outer strap of each flip-flop, with the bead in the center of the flower and the leaves on either side, as shown in the diagram below

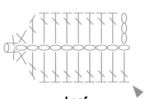

Leaf
foundation chain = 10 chs
(make 4 in green)

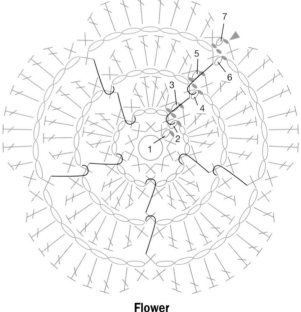

Flower
(make 2 in orange)

⤬ back post single crochet in this stitch (so that the petals formed by the earlier rounds remain on the front of the flower)

BIRTHDAY PARTY

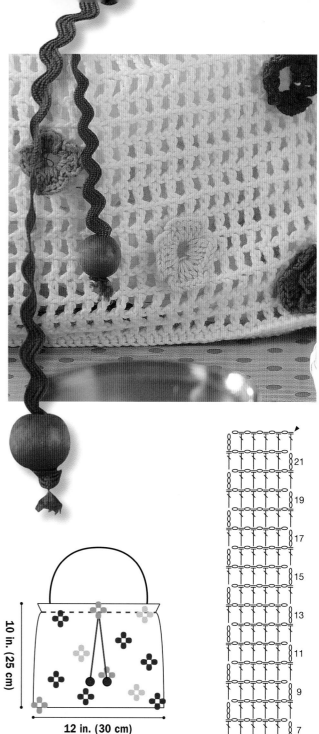

YARN: Superfine (weight category 1) cotton yarn, 2 skeins (each 150 yd/137 m; 1.76 oz./50 g) in white, 1 each in red, green, orange, and fuchsia

HOOK: U.S. size D-3 (3.25 mm) crochet hook

NOTIONS: 1 yd. (0.9 m) fuchsia rickrack trim; 2 fuchsia wooden beads; 2 clear plastic handles, 12 in. (30 cm) long and 1/10 in. (3 mm) thick

FINISHED MEASUREMENTS: 12 by 10 in. (30 by 25 cm); 1¾ in. (4.5 cm) deep

GAUGE: 27 sts and 11 rows = 4 by 4 in. (10 by 10 cm)

PATTERN

BACK

With white, ch 75.

Row 1: Dc tbl in sixth ch from hook. *Ch 1, sk 1 ch, dc tbl in next ch; rep from * across. Turn. **Rows 2–22:** Ch 3 (counts as first dc), *ch 1, sk 1 st, dc tbl in next st; rep from * across. Turn. Fasten off.

FRONT

Work same as back.

SIDE (MAKE 2)

With white, ch 15.

Row 1: Dc tbl in sixth ch from hook. *Ch 1, sk 1 ch, dc tbl in next ch; rep from * across. Turn. **Rows 2–22:** Ch 3 (counts as first dc), *ch 1, sk 1 st, dc tbl in next st; rep from * across. Turn. Fasten off.

BOTTOM

With white, ch 74.

Row 1: Dc in second ch from hook and in each ch across. Turn. **Rows 2–4:** Ch 3 (counts as first dc), dc in each st across. Fasten off.

FLOWER

Join yarn in any opening on front of bag. On each side of opening (the ch above and below and the dc post on either side), work [ch 3, 3 dc, ch 3, sl st]. Fasten off.

Work 4 flowers in fuchsia, 3 in green, 3 in orange, and 2 in red, scattered randomly across the front of the bag.

FINISHING

Attach the front, back, bottom, and sides of the bag together by working a row of single crochet along each seam, working through both layers of fabric. Weave the rickrack through the bag near the top edge, pull to tighten, and tie loosely. Attach the beads to the ends of the rickrack. Sew the handles to the bag with white yarn.

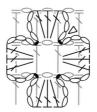

10 in. (25 cm)

12 in. (30 cm)

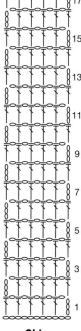

Flower
make 4 in fuchsia
3 in green
3 in orange
2 in red

Side
foundation chain = 11 chs
(make 2 in white)

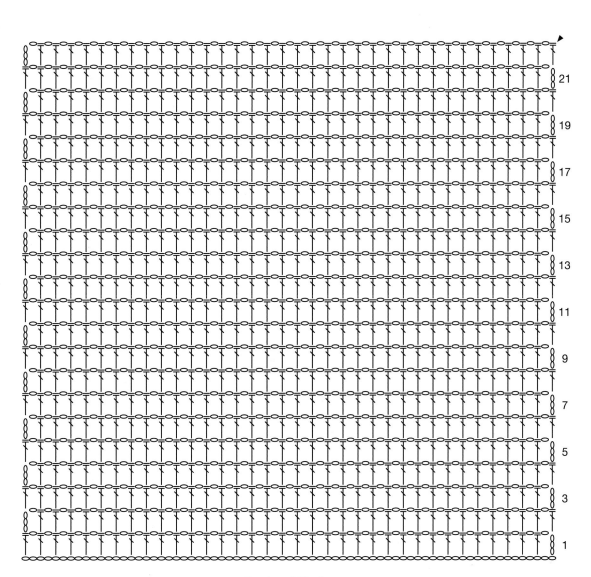

Front and Back
foundation chain = 71 chs
(make 2 in white)

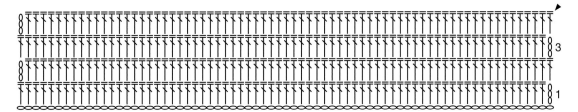

Bottom
foundation chain = 71 chs
(make 1 in white)

dc tbl: work a double crochet, inserting the hook under only the back loop of the stitch of the previous row

TEAK

YARN: Superfine (weight category 1) cotton yarn, 2 skeins (each 150 yd/137 m; 1.76 oz./50 g) in ecru, 1 in green
HOOK: U.S. size G-6 (4.0 mm) crochet hook
FINISHED MEASUREMENTS: 5½ by 6 in. (14 by 15 cm)
GAUGE: 24 sts and 15 rows = 4 by 4 in. (10 by 10 cm)

PATTERN

With two strands of ecru held together, ch 37. (Work with two strands of yarn held together throughout the pattern.)
Row 1: Dc in 4th ch from hook and in each ch across. Turn. **Rows 2–3:** With green, ch 1, sc in each st across. Turn. **Rows 4–5:** With ecru, ch 3 (counts as first dc), dc in each st across. Turn. **Rows 6–7:** Repeat Rows 2–3. **Rows 8–43:** Repeat Rows 4–7. **Rows 44–55:** Continue as indicated in the stitch chart. Fasten off.

ASSEMBLY

Fold the piece in half with the right side of the fabric on the inside, lining up the green stripes and work a row of single crochet through both layers of fabric around the sides and bottom of the piece to join the front and back together. Turn the purse right side out.

STRAP

With two strands of ecru held together, ch 6.
Row 1: Dc in 4th ch from hook and in last ch. Turn. **Row 2:** Ch 3 (counts as first dc), dc in each st across. Turn. Repeat Row 2 until strap measures about 1 yd. (0.9 m). Fasten off. Sew the ends of the strap to either side of the top edge of the bag.

BUTTON

With two strands of green held together, ch 4, join with a sl st to form a ring.
Round 1: Ch 3 (counts as first dc), work 5 dc in ring, join with sl st in 3rd ch of beg ch-3. **Round 2:** Ch 1, sc2tog 3 times, join with a sl st in beg ch.

Fasten off, leaving a tail of about 4 in. (10 cm). Thread the tail through the sts of the last row and pull tight, then fasten off and cut the yarn, hiding the end inside of the button. Sew the button to the front of the bag where the buttonhole at the end of the flap falls.

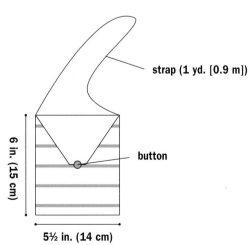

strap (1 yd. [0.9 m])

button

6 in. (15 cm)

5½ in. (14 cm)

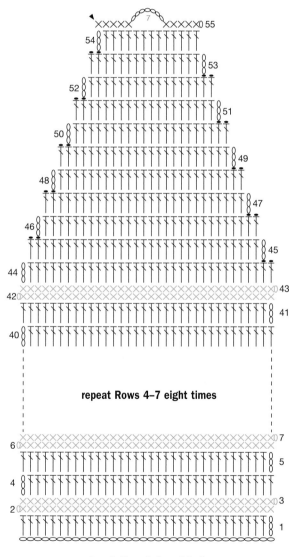

repeat Rows 4–7 eight times

foundation chain = 34 chs

GREEN TEA

Turn the piece upside down and join the yarn at the bottom edge as shown on the stitch chart. Working in the unused loops of the foundation chain, repeat Rows 58–66 on the lower part of the bag. Fasten off.

FINISHING

Place the handles at either end of the piece, fold the flaps down, and sew them in place with small stitches. Fold the bag in half and sew the side seams.

YARN: Superfine (weight category 1) cotton yarn, 4 skeins (each 150 yd/137 m; 1.76 oz./50 g) in green
HOOK: U.S. size G-6 (4.0 mm) crochet hook
NOTIONS: 2 bamboo handles
FINISHED MEASUREMENTS: 13 by 8 in. (32 by 20 cm)
GAUGE: 20 sts and 15 rows = 4 by 4 in. (10 by 10 cm)

PATTERN

With 2 strands of yarn held together (here and throughout), ch 69.
Row 1: Sc in second ch from hook and in each ch across. Turn.
Row 2: Ch 3 (counts as first dc), dc in each st across. Turn. **Row 3:** Ch 1, sc in each st across. Turn. **Rows 4–57:** Repeat Rows 2–3. **Rows 58–66:** Continue as indicated in the stitch chart. Fasten off.

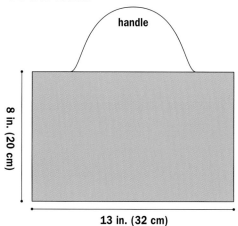

handle

8 in. (20 cm)

13 in. (32 cm)

fold these 3 flaps down over the handle

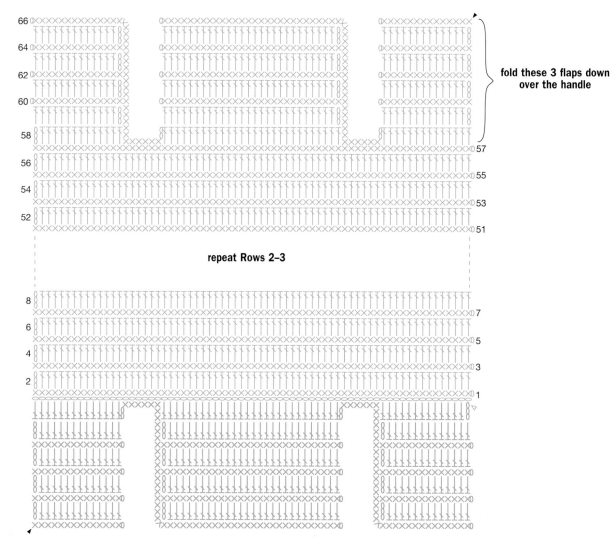

repeat Rows 2–3

foundation chain = 68 chs

PLUM

YARN: Superfine (weight category 1) cotton yarn, 14 skeins (each 150 yd/137 m; 1.76 oz./50 g) in brick red, 2 skeins in bright red

HOOK: U.S. size G-6 (6.0 mm) crochet hook

NOTIONS: Yarn needle; sturdy cardboard; fabric for lining: 1 piece 10 by 5½ in. (25 by 14 cm) and 1 piece 24 by 12 in. (61 by 30 cm)

FINISHED MEASUREMENTS: 9 in. (23 cm) wide and 10 in. (25 cm) tall

GAUGE: 5 pattern repeats and 16 rows in fantasy stitch = 8 by 8 in. (20 by 20 cm)

PATTERN BOTTOM

With two strands of brick red held together, ch 9. Work 10 rounds of single crochet around the chain, increasing as indicated in the stitch chart.

SIDES

Continue around the piece in fantasy stitch (see key below), with 14 repetitions of the stitch in each round, for 26 rounds. Next work 4 rnds of sc (with 70 sts in each round); finally, work a rnd of rev sc, as indicated in the stitch chart.

FINISHING

With 2 strands of bright red yarn, embroider 6 columns of cross stitch on the bag, spacing them out around the bag as shown. Crochet the handle as shown in the diagram. Sew the ends of the handle to the inside top edge of the bag. Cut a piece of cardboard in an oval just smaller than the bottom of the bag, and place it in the bottom of the bag. Slide the lining inside the bag and sew it to the bag around the bottom and around the top edge, using the lining to hide the ends of the handle. Make a twisted cord from bright red yarn and thread it through the openings in the last row of fantasy stitch.

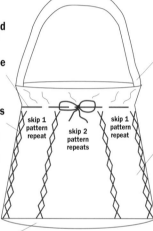

Drawstring: Make a twisted cord from 5½ yd. (5 m) of bright red yarn. Thread it through the openings in the last row of fantasy stitch.

Embroider 6 columns of cross stitch (with 2 strands of bright red yarn) on the sides of the bag, leaving the last row of fantasy stitch free for the drawstring.

skip 1 pattern repeat

skip 2 pattern repeats

skip 1 pattern repeat

Sew the ends of the handle to the inside top edge of the bag before attaching the lining.

Line the inside of the bag with 2 rectangles of fabric, one 10 by 5½ in. (25 by 14 cm) and the other 24 by 12 in. (61 by 30 cm).

fantasy stitch: sc in next st, stretch out the loop on the hook, skip 3 sts, [dc, ch 1, dc] in next st

∨ **work 2 sc in the same st**

⩔ **work 3 sc in the same stitch**

Cut an oval 9 by 4 in. (23 by 10 cm) from sturdy cardboard and place it in the bottom of the bag before attaching the lining.

Handle: Work a row of half double crochet with brick red around 14 strands of yarn, 20 in. (51 cm) long.

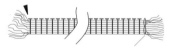

Sew the ends securely so that the stitches don't unravel.

Note: In Round 11, space the 14 pattern repeats out evenly around the bag.

Bag

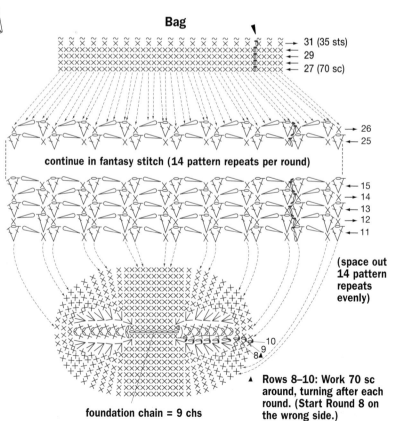

→ 31 (35 sts)
← 29
← 27 (70 sc)

→ 26
→ 25

continue in fantasy stitch (14 pattern repeats per round)

→ 15
→ 14
→ 13
→ 12
→ 11

(space out 14 pattern repeats evenly)

10
9
8

foundation chain = 9 chs

▲ **Rows 8–10: Work 70 sc around, turning after each round. (Start Round 8 on the wrong side.)**